# Heart Island

# Heart Island

*Stephen Cushman* (signature)

Poems by Stephen Cushman

*David Robert Books*

To the Davies,
with warm wishes +
gratitude.
Steve
11/26/06

Published by David Robert Books
P.O. Box 541106
Cincinnati, OH 45254-1106

Typeset in Garamond by WordTech Communications LLC,
Cincinnati, OH

ISBN: 1933456353
LCCN: 2006930724

Poetry Editor: Kevin Walzer
Business Editor: Lori Jareo

Visit us on the web at www.davidrobertbooks.com

# Acknowledgments

*Alabama Literary Review*: "June"; "Semele"; "September";
    "White Rainbow"
*Archipelago*: "Another Anniversary of Appomattox";
    "December"; "May"
*Connecticut Review*: "Night Sky over Norwalk, 1956";
    "Rhythm Section"; "Selenitic"
*Cortland Review*: "Between Blackfriars and Waterloo"
*CUE: A Journal of Prose Poetry*: "My Father's Study"
*Drunken Boat*: "Extispicious"; "January"; "March"
*English Journal*: "Chador"
*Free Verse*: "Surveillance"
*Iron Horse Literary Review*: "If Augustine Could Ride the
    Hammersmith and City Line"
*ISLE (Interdisciplinary Studies in Literature and the
    Environment)*: "Berries and Buds"; "Divine Wind"
*Meridian*: "After the Memorial Service"
*Smartish Pace*: "Blueberry Gun"; "Shoulder Season";
    "Bioluminescence Is a Big Word"; "In the Pharisee's
    House"; "Mending"; "April"
*South Carolina Review*: "Crush"; "Dido and the Arrow";
    "Heart Island"; "Hocus Pocus"; "Hornet's Nest";
    "Intimate"
*Southwest Review*: "Marthe Removing Her Nightdress in the
    Garden at Montval"; "Eurasian Eagle Owl"
*Tampa Review*: "The Murderer's Hand"
*Yale Review*: "Behind Closed Doors"

*For Biggy, who first took us there.*

# Contents

# January

What a scam.
Throw us back a few scraps of light
for our emaciated afternoons,

and without an almanac no one will know
you carved that light
off darker mornings.

If I could illuminate
a new Book of Hours,
I'd skip the Circumcision,

pass up Epiphany, even drop
the Confession of Peter
and Conversion of Paul

to draw cartoons of all
the nitwits in t-shirts
who think your thaw

means beans and is
a merciful beneficence
granted in the coldest month

rather than the sadist's ruse
to lull as we resume the plough,
then lash us raw.

You're namesake of the god of gates.
So what. Two-faced is two-faced.
I like you least. And sometimes hate.

# Hornet's Nest

Though some resemble basketballs,
this gray bolus of chewed-up wood
and flora fiber hanging from
a leafless branch has only grown
as big as a human head,

which might look, to a certain kind
of eye that opens back into
a certain kind of mind, something like
a traitor's head hung up to warn
the rest of us against transgressions.

From there how small a step it is
to thoughts of great decapitations,
Medusa, John the Baptist, Mary,
Queen of Scots, and suddenly that's that,
since despite all good intentions

this kind of mind has once again
imposed itself where it doesn't belong
and has no business butting in
to tie the January sky
up with a baldfaced hornets' nest.

Gray sky, gray tree, gray branch, gray nest
a certain kind of mind can do
anything to but leave it alone,
even compare it, the colorless
paper clod suspended high

off the ground, to a somber piñata
for knocking down in celebration
of hornets as papermakers, of queens
who mate and flee to hibernate
in protected locations, of males

left behind to freeze with first frost,
the nest, which hornets don't inhabit
longer than a single season,
become a flimsy mausoleum
of stings and venom and lives that went with them.

# Dido and the Arrow

*Like a doe pierced with an arrow.*
But what can Virgil really know

about this widow, queen of Carthage,
about the ways she has to manage

her desire, there in the bed with her
ornate headboard brought from Tyre

when she fled bereaved, now pushed
close to the window, as if she wished

passersby to see its carvings
and fantasize about her starving

flesh on purple sheets, though in fact
she never in her life has lacked

strategies for sublimation.
How else could she have risen

to power or run the city so well?
Virgil thinks it goes to hell

when she gets horny, no more work
on the half-built towers in the dark

heat of her distraction. Oh, come on.
People have stuff to do and function

just fine, thank you. They can't moon
their lives away, so pretty soon

they learn about infatuation,
how it's better not to listen

when they keep playing that song,
how pretty soon there's nothing wrong

working harder cannot fix,
and if there is, we've got ethics

to don in most colors and sizes.
Our wounds have so many disguises

to choose from that we seldom throw
ourselves on swords like Virgil's Dido,

who for all we know caressed
the arrow sticking in her breast

and fingered its fletching each night,
perhaps intending to excite

herself to sleep with notch and feathers,
with unmet need that has its pleasures.

# Accumulation

All night
quiet snow,
then with morning
a change to sleet
and lots of little
lovers lobbing
frozen pebbles
at my window.

# February

Despite the shearing of days,
two or three clipped from your rump,
you're the black sheep of months,
a brand new year already old,
its recent thaw forgotten in cold
northwest wind that spikes the air
and makes it hard to feel
even absent chiggers, ticks, snakes
reimburse for chapped lips, sere skin,
furnace-baked throat.
                              No wonder we need
groundhog prophecy, deciphering shadows
we see all around for clues to the future,
though winter, prolonged or abbreviated,
still centers in you. As for Lent,
you're perfect. What else is there to do
but fast and repent? And yet, it's true.
I have to admit a soft spot for you.
Without your ancient festival, how would I,
a black sheep, too,
know when it's time to purify?

# The Murderer's Hand

takes mine and squeezes

its white fingers tight,
like a blood-warm glove

one size too small,
but that grip, his grasp,

helps take the chill
off the windowless library

of a county jail,
our Sunday circle

of men in stripes
and me in a tie

all bowing heads
to heat we can't see.

# Into the Pharisee's House

*(Luke 7:36)*

Those feet, for all the dust
And dirt between the toes
Stubbed on a temple stair,

Those feet still made me want
To fall on my knees and kiss
Each slender ankle, heel,

Uncalloused arch that leaves
No print wherever it treads,
Never touching our earth.

Tears? How could I help them
Or keep myself from crying
Harder when I saw

My droplets clearing paths
Along his skin? Nothing
From my mischievous body

Washed anything clean before,
So, left then right both rinsed,
Of course I had to use

My hair, black and softer
Than any cloth, and next
The alabaster flask:

What else could I have chosen
Except my precious unguent

To salve the sandalless flesh

And show how much I love
Now that I have so much
More for him to forgive?

# Black Ice

If only it lived
up to its name,
it wouldn't be quite
as terribly hazardous,
but sheets and patches
of perfect purity
can kill by coating
so very clearly
that surfaces show
their truest colors.

# Let Her Rip

Back to square one with another rookie month
and questions of coping, and right from the git-go
the hollow fills up with cinders of snow,
shutting in the widow with her own whitened porch.

Not much on first impressions, are we, March?
Schools closed, planes delayed, the roads to work
all paved with physics lessons, how bodies in motion
quickly behave without strictures of friction.

But if monks in the desert disparaged disparagement,
let me try, too, though they skipped the penance
involving snow, to keep in mind that as you sweep
this mess up with the sun, you give me back,
according to the almanac, more light than anyone.

# March

It's true you're no beauty,
splotchy complexion, not much hair,
and your greatest achievement, an equinox,
barely breaks even when you're two-thirds through.
Yes, a few daffodils, but it's also true
your moodiness gets tiresome,
one day the bluebirds going berserk
with amorous gurgling aroused by your warmth,
the next a cold shoulder, ice on the birdbath,
all desire dead. Your name suggests
aggressive designs, maybe a strategy,
in these sudden fluctuations;
yet notwithstanding the frost-stunned forsythia,
your name's a misnomer for the month that means
steady improvement and annually moves
from worse to bad, bad to better,
going the way not everything does.

# Hocus Pocus

Smartly dressed, dashing commuter,
from your tailored sleeve you've lost
this button, large and yellow, torn off
in the jostled rush and rolling still
across the platform as you leap aboard
between closing doors before I can manage
to snap it up, overtake you, and return
what now I know I'll never see mended,

so what else can I do, now that you're gone,
but carry your token wherever I go
to charm away all curses, hexes,
evil spells, like the one of believing
every story must have sides, and yours,
belonging to you alone, can never be mine?

# Between Blackfriars and Waterloo

In a country that dreads most color
it looks so loud against the mud,

black mud and red blanket spread
by the edge of the shriveled Thames

as strollers crowd the Queen's Walk
to lean on a railing and study the scene:

two policewomen in black caps,
white shirts, neckties, two guys

in huge rubber boots dredging the shallows,
pewter clouds overhead that let the sun

leak on the mud through cracks of blue,
and under the blanket something uncovered

by outgoing tide, somebody's body
shrouded in my favorite color.

# Austromantic

Weathercock, windsock,
One wet finger in the air,
As though direction mattered much
And wind meant nothing more
Than rain today, sun tomorrow;
As though to know the wind
By where it comes from
Or the speed it blows would be to know
More than any pilot knows, any sailor,
Farmer, dog, and what is what they know
Of air in all its motions
Compared to knowing it by touch
Against the cheek or neck,
By exhalations in the ear
Or ways it plays through someone's hair?

# April

Ecstasy's a must, not a luxury,
especially after an abstemious season,
a regimen of penitence, its cold snaps
of self-denial finally yielding
to an abstinent ear completely swacked
on cardinal song, an undefiled eye
helplessly wild for weeping cherry,
its photographed fountain of ravishing pink.
Forsythia, redbud, spirea, pear,
each desire known and none unrequited,
but best of all, it doesn't last,
since ecstasy's a discipline, too,
a severe austerity that mortifies boredom,
fasts away irony, flagellates cool.
Lucky it's brief, or it'd be lethal.

# Ophiomantic

Bluebirds, redbuds, the world's in heat,
and in town bare legs and feet
have blossomed in the parks, in gardens,
in public places where temperance depends
on blindness alone. But out here
there's more than just feathers and flowers
and flesh; out here the latest news
is snakes are moving, too, so it's better
to wear shoes, the first one, black,
startled Saturday, like a dark tongue licking
chapped lips of rock while making sounds
so few will find pleasing, the sounds of wind
already bothering these oncoming leaves.

# Semele

*Come to me as you come to her.*
Poor girl, pregnant and in the heat
of wanting to know her lover a god,

wheedles from him the promised favor
that can only mean the end of her
seismic skin and resonant lips.

*Come to me as you come to her,*
queen of heaven with studded scepter
unable to conceive and fixed

on seeing this fertile rival
across the Styx into total blackness
where he will never hope to follow,

having come as she insisted
in the fullness of a fire
no human can withstand and overwhelmed

her hummingbird heart, its seizure
complete before the coupling
cremated her, still warm, and left him

alone to carry their issue,
holy, intoxicating offspring,
sewn up close inside him.

# A Spanish Day

Today is Monday and April, and I'm in Madrid
in the Plaza de España, and there is much sun.

I only speak a little Spanish
and don't know words for many things
like one for the sky when it's easy to see.

Like the sky today, a day to say things
only in Spanish because I want to learn quickly
but also because what I can't say in Spanish
I don't need to say. Not today.

Today is Monday and April, and I'm in Madrid
in the Plaza de España, and there is much sun,

maybe too much when someone drinks wine
and not enough water, but the wine is good

and the sun is good, and here is Cervantes,
a monument for him, and here are two statues,
Quixote and Sancho, and I only speak a little Spanish

and don't know words for many things
like the ones for the time that isn't now.

I am not drinking the tinted wine now.
I am drinking the tinted wine earlier.
Now I'm drinking nothing, and I'm not in the sun
because the sun is too much and is there in the sky
when it's easy to see.

I'm not in the sun, and I'm near the old men
and don't know the word for where there's no sun,
but that's where we are, and the old men say nothing
and look towards Cervantes because that's where they are,
the young in the sun with good hands and feet
and many other things I don't know the words for.

The old men say nothing, and their silence is good
like water that's cold when the sun is too much,
and it's true I'm not old, but I'm also not young.

Not today. Today is Monday and April,
and Enchanted, I say, to the Plaza de España,
to Madrid and the sun and the easy-see sky

because I only speak a little Spanish
and Enchanted is the thing to say
when you see someone for the very first time,
and when he says, Good Afternoon, How Are You,
I Call Myself Cervantes, I can say
Enchanted, Cervantes, I Am Very Well,
I Call Myself Esteban, and then we are friends
and can drink the tinted wine together
in the sun with the sky in the Plaza de España.

But not today. I only speak a little Spanish
and do not know in the Plaza de España
that when I'm in the hotel again,
without Cervantes and the silent old men,

the señora is saying your mother is calling
and here is the number and then it's the night
for my father forever and he's without sun
or water or wine, and now he's enchanted
on Monday in April far from Madrid.

# Another Anniversary of Appomattox

Some people so lonely
they can't bear the birds again,
those catchy solos about duets
mouthing off outside the window.

Others been lonely so long
they're used to making do
and don't want you
reminding them of redbud blossoms

they've learned to live without.
So if you're a victor, shut
your trap and do no harm
to people who hear in birds,

this wren,
only the terms of surrender.

# May

So subjunctive, your name;
yet there's nothing iffy
about the trees in basic green,

their colorful underwear gone
back in the drawer of early spring,
nothing the least bit contingent

in the way a wood thrush succeeds
white-throated sparrows at dawn
or iris follows dogwood.

Here in the northern temperate zone,
how could you possibly express
the hypothetical, the wish,

with all your satisfactions
so relentlessly indicative?
Oh, what I wouldn't give

to cross your looks with just a whiff
of that autumnal musk
you emanate down under.

# Bioluminescence Is a Big Word

for tiny cells and tissues
fermenting with an enzyme
inside the abdomen of the very first firefly

this spring, the only one floating
above the dark acres of a derelict farm
on a muggy May evening. Could be a scout

charged by the others with patrolling the fields,
in bad need of mowing, for non-flying females
on the ground or in bushes, who seeing him beam

the correct species signal, answer right back
in codes of their own. Or maybe he's eager,
this soft-bodied beetle, and impressively potent.

Whatever the case, how can they call
a device for mating *heatless light*?
And why dub him lightning bug

when his guttering glow has less in common
with blinding bolts than blinking yellow
at midnight intersections, *caution, caution*

flashed out here against the black
to steady the pulse in spite of all risk
inherent in chemistry, no matter how small.

# Shoulder Season

A sea-side town in Greece
and on the way back from the beach,

along a lane beside the train tracks
through groves of groaning lemon trees

and stands of red poppies,
past purple quilts of bougainvillea

and one sparrow with a currant in its beak
and something heard in the uncut grass

with too much slither for a lizard,
a middle-aged man out trying to teach

himself to ride a beat-up bicycle,
to learn on a few wobbly turns of the pedals

the secret of balance,
having no father to show him how

between the crashes of metal that sound
down the lane at regular intervals

across the warming Gulf of Corinth
from the snowy peak of Parnassus.

# Selenitic

Said of a flower
that opens in moonshine,

but doesn't it mean
full moon bamboozles

the gullible flower,
counterfeiting sun

by cranking out shadows,
or does such a flower

discriminate between
any old onslaught

of usable beams
and the moon's special mix

of darkness and light
pressure, tender

yet insistent
as it coaxes each petal

so ready to open
to just the right touch.

# June

You probably thought it enough to be
        the lightest month of the year
        and wear your solstice like a sign

of royalty, a diadem of early dawns,
        games outside or aimless strolls
        after dinner, children tucked in

before rooms go dark. You've always been
        the most desired (you know it's true)
        by pupils and teachers, and I suppose

all that yearning goes to your head
        with the annual fuss made over you
        by brides and grooms, named as you are

for the goddess of marriage.
                    But now don't you see
        not everybody likes you, whether it be
        the allergy-wracked, for whom you're misery,

the farmer or gardener who seethes
        under drought, or the introverted night owl
        your thoughtless radiance has trespassed against.

As for brides and grooms, it depends,
        I guess, on how much a marriage,
        with each anniversary, takes after Juno's,

which one should celebrate in songs
        that rhyme you not with *tune* or *moon*
        but with *lampoon, typhoon, spittoon.*

# Blueberry Gun

All the summers and still it startles,
the first shot fired over fields of blue fruit
sweetening above the sea since June
along with its echo around the bay
as vulnerable bushes discharge their birds
into ripening air, bushes that redden
hillsides in fall and birds there to dine
on the lucrative berries. All the summers
and still it puzzles, this question of who
gets to fire the gun and whether it's loaded
with birdshot or blanks. Is it triggered
by machine at automatic intervals,
or does someone in overalls rip off each blast
before he starts harvesting? After all
the summers it should be obvious
what kind of tactics will scatter black
thoughts as the gun scatters birds.

# White Rainbow

A trick
Of heavy fog
Blanketing our hollow
While from blue sky above a ridge
The sun

Glosses
Floating droplets
That somehow glow and bend
The light in one translucent arc
Like this.

*You are*
*At the center*
*Of each rainbow you see,*
Says my encyclopedia.
Uh-o.

A ghost,
An albino,
No prismatic spectrum:
What kind of covenant is that?
Soothe me

Again;
Say the center
Hasn't lost all color;
Say, We're richer unrefracted,
Aren't we?

# If Augustine Could Ride the Hammersmith and City Line

Suppose one tries to mortify sight
by walking the streets with lowered eyes,
never glancing to the left or right,

and winds up swaying in the crowded aisle
of a train at rush hour unable to see
anything but a pair of perfect legs

crossed squarely in the field of vision?
What then? Rather than pluck them out
and throw them down on the dirty floor,

does one simply shut the eyes, like children
at a monster movie, or do we cool the blood
by reciting the names of seven muscles

that make up the calf, the fleshy part
at the back of the leg whose pregnant curve
bears little resemblance to sources of veal,

much less to a newborn elephant or whale,
but hints instead at something—
where were we? Right, the seven muscles,

chief among them *gastrocnemius*,
a name that sounds as though a stomach
should be involved, and maybe it is

if the original namer saw this muscle
belly out behind the shinbone
rounded with a power it gives her

to wiggle her toes inside her shoes,
black and leather with medium heels,
or to lift her body on the balls of her feet

each time she—or is the trick
to let the eyes slip off their leash
and rise above the sheer white hosiery

to the larger picture that includes her lap,
the hardbound book she's reading on it,
and the stunted hand that holds it open,

a fingerless fist, which in lieu of digits
has tumorous stubs, a few pink
balloons she's never used to point

or beckon or wear a ring upon,
pink as this line on the underground map
that lattices the city, its many entwinings.

# Chador

I believe in submission and want to be one
who submits, despite the blue skin of the sky,
with joy to obligation, one who can fast
through deserts of years without thirst
for a single forbidden sip. I also believe
in the final revelation and want to accept
the total cloaking from head to toe
for modesty and my own protection,
but what do I do when I go abroad
behind a black veil, my share of creation
only the stripe I can see through its slit,
with this infidel wishing for wind in my hair,
the heretic sun on my shoulders and arms,
the blaspheming earth beneath my bare feet?

# Eurasian Eagle Owl with Ambulance

The sign says Dangerous Animal
and shows a hand with severed pinkie,

but who can blame a nocturnal creature
for acting crabby at this early hour,

big, brindled body perched on a branch
as the leopard head swivels to let orange eyes,

which cannot move on their own in sockets,
follow so closely the movements of morning.

Just like a cat's its tufted ears twitch
to the increasing chorus of neighboring cries,

the screech, the squawk, the soloist caw,
exotic, unknown, and this loud howl

that comes with captivity and sours to flatness
the moment it passes.

# July

Sinner that I am, I confess
I'd sin more if not for you,
annual overdose of uncut sun
and Roman reminder, not so friendly,
of flames one never can snuff or douse,
burning lake and raining brimstone
of which you are the shot I down
each time I climb in the furnace,
the black interior baked all day
in a treeless lot, windows sealed,
your little hit of hell, which warns
away from pride and dangerous delusion
that you can immunize against the infernal.

# Pyromantic

Blue-tipped kitchen match,
Teach me how to strike
Anywhere and flare beyond
The reach of children, teach me
How to burn without burning
Up or down or out.

# Intimate

The new moon rises
always at sunrise,
invisible, empty,
contributing nothing
to canine lunacy
or crimes committed
in city streets, and yet
for all its hiding
in total darkness,
for all the secrecy
imposed by daylight,
a new moon pushes
high tides higher,
flooding the features
we usually see
as cryptic gravity
meanwhile tugs
low tides lower,
exposing parts
we usually don't.

# Rhythm Section

So many percussings:
woodpecker clatter
against a dead oak,
a cloudburst's tattoo
on hickory leaves,
a knock at the door
by the long-lost knuckle
of a hand often held.
No wonder the drum's
oldest of instruments
when so much consists
of constantly striking
the stretched heads of nerves
and bewildering needs.
Makes sense that somebody
would yearn to transform
beating and battering
into resonant texture
while leaving another
the niceties of notes,
the privilege of melody.

# Heart Island

No metaphor
but a real place on the chart
just offshore.
Shaped like a heart?

Not exactly, and the books
don't say how they came,
these trees and rocks,
to have this name,

rising from the bay
as dark green dome
where a nesting osprey
makes its home

and scolds intruders
with sharp whistles, frenzied
above dead firs,
angry at our need

to land and climb again
around high meadow
where we were children,
at our wish to throw

ourselves once more from cliffs
into numbing ocean
and burn away *what ifs*,
*if onlys* from the skin,

to shade ourselves in spruce
festooned with hanging moss
and not think *It's no use*
or focus on the loss,

to pick again the raspberries,
which look and taste like lips
mostly kissed in fantasies,
those pure relationships.

# August

King of the months, and in his mane
rose hips ripen, fireweed ignites,

as each day dots a red i of sunset
and rubricates the bay. Sprawled in his paws,

rough tongue licking sea salt from us,
we don't always notice the punctual oaks

start to disseminate, their acorn hail
a nuisance underfoot for us,

but for red squirrels, whose chatter revs
higher than falsetto outboards,

it's time to gather more than rosebuds.
More power to them, amidst abundance

anticipating want; hats off to those
lounging between the fuzzy paws

still mindful of retractable claws.

# Extispicious

Fight or flight is not the only choice.
There's also *freeze*, as in *Be still and know*
catching a predator's eye can mean
fangs at the throat, claws in the belly.
So let's be still. Still as a squirrel
on the limb of an oak when in the next tree
a red-tailed hawk eviscerates a neighbor,
or maybe a mate, in its own leafy nest,
ripping gray fur away from the meat,
gulping it down, careless of bones,
while even to blink or wince or cringe,
when witnessing this, with tail curled tight,
is to be next on the list for talons and beak.

# Surveillance

So many cameras
ready for holdups,
those who shoplift,
and the stoplight runner;
yet for all the tape
that rolls without ceasing,
where's the evidence,
the footage that catches
one in the act,
bareassed, redhanded,
of breaking down love,
as flora does sunlight,
into something unseen
that still can sustain?

# My Sister's Watch

keeps its own sweet time,
quarter to lilac, half-past apple tree,
sugar maple sharp, and makes time fly
now like a heron, Great Blue loping
with folded neck and trailing legs, now
like a fish hawk already rising
from the talon-punctured sea. Waterproof,
yes, or at least enough to shed any tears,
while at night its dial, aglow in green,
presses a luminous face to hers.
Three sweeping hands patrol her cheek.
What makes them tick, the hidden works
behind the crystal, scored and cracked
by spills she's taken on foggy rocks?
Not much mystery for an average watchmaker.
What about her, though, the one who wears it
to keep appointments she's always making?
What about someone unspoken, disguised,
with whom she's secretly synchronized?

# September

Most sedative lunation,
let you be a lesson to me,
wild oats sown,
                    killer heat cooled,
and the shock of first frost
not so close yet.
                    With scads
of air-conditioners hushed at last
and furnaces still fireless,
a window opens as cicadas finally
mute into remission,
                    easing up
that strident static in favor of
relaxing crickets.
                    You're the state
philosophy fantasizes,
                    the golden mean
medication emulates,
                    your serene repose
a balancing act of light and dark
that never goes overboard,
                    though just offshore
tropic storms stall,
                    hurricanes roar.

# After Curfew

Ridgeline silhouette
in partial moonlight
and in the bottom land
blackened below
something's vaguely
different or wrong
or let's say anomalous
in the sound of night
after days of rain
after months of drought,
which dried the creek
now suddenly back
without hoopla or fanfare
to speak in tongues
all but forgotten
and sing of things
first lost, then missed,
then no longer noticed.

# Crush

What would a psychiatrist say
about this achy love of the sky?
Or how diagnose the anxious flutter
when clouds close in from the western horizon?

That in fact it can't be love at all,
since love depends on knowing and who can know
the sky, the clouds, or things so remote
as solstice sun and distant stars?

That in fact it's only infatuation,
the regressive return to ecstatic merging
with mother in infancy, a blissful state
of illusory union, a total collapse of ego

boundaries, a phase in mating behavior
that's temporary and must be or else
those humans would die of never eating
and never sleeping and always shaking

beholding the beloved, and then the work,
who would do it, raising children,
burying parents? Well, of course;
yet just the same, how blue, how blue

and how the windows in a little house
somewhere under all that blue can rattle
with neither sonic boom nor thunder
but undone sobbing long overdue.

# Divine Wind

Is the buck that charges
a car on the interstate,

ramming his rack
through the driver's-side door

so antlers catch and his neck
snaps instantly,

quixotic casualty
or kamikaze in ecstasy?

# October

the one i think the world of
and now that you're finally here
with red-lip leaves and blue-eye sky
i'm shy and can no more say
*sweetie* or *snookums* to your
blonde noons after drenching dews
than i could pull myself away
from your colorful skin far enough
to say *oriency* or name
the way you lace the warm with cool
long-awaited *frescade* of the year
or admit i know my mind will go
if i cannot basiate you

# Deciduous

Ash tree, losing leaves first
from the bottom up as always,
what do you do for me?

Darken the circles under my eyes;
sharpen the outlines of my ribs
and my pelvis; make my chest feel

too small for a heart.
Is it any wonder
I love you

October after October
when you lift your mottled frock
up the trunk to your shoulders

and over your distant head
and deepen all I do?

# Mending

Here candidates squabble,
There a government topples,
And farther off our forces
Go on high alert;

Yet even though
I can sew we sit
Side by side, you stitching
Buttons back on my blue shirt.

# November

In an old field nobody mows
red cedars take over,
their conical heads widened with age

and this time of year their scaly foliage
breaking out in bluish fruit
the graying tinge of Roquefort mold.

Despite the juniper
in their Latin name,
we'd probably go blind
from gin we tried making.
As if drinking would help.

Besides, birds eat the berries
and, perching on the rusted wire
of slackened fences, pass the seeds,
which grow new trees, defining the fence line,

as I hope you,
month that's not my first choice,
will pass me through your darkened tract,
afternoon gone and guns all around,
and sow me one more time.

# Marthe Removing Her Nightdress in the Garden at Montval

Bonnard has jacked the contrast up so high in this
        photograph
it might as well be moonless, starless midnight
for all the garden we can see to the left or right
beyond the tree she's facing. What light she has
comes from behind and hoods the head with shadow,
almost turning her naked trunk into one of those
decapitated torsos from Greece or Rome.
There's no denying the classic back and nice butt;
yet first prize for whiteness goes to the nightdress,
the white made whiter by enabling black.
Frankly, though, even the dress takes runner-up
to your changing hair, the rivulet
that starts with the part, streaking the scalp,
then swells to freshet, spate, and finally with age
becomes wild water some might skip for a fountain
        of youth
but I will love to chug and guzzle.

# Lip Service

How inadequate the consolations:
*Could be worse, Count your blessings,*
*Think of people who are starving.*
Glib, facile, fatuous, inane,
in no way denting or faintly easing
the specter of having to pass his room
when it's empty. Forever. And how
pathetic the language of gratitude
when news is good, the lump benign
*(Much obliged! Thanks a bunch!),*
as just like that the sorry-ass
days of an autumn past its prime
erupt in beautyberry, making it
impossible to see the colorless woods
for all the violet clusters shining
in cold, gray rain, each drop a kiss,
the kind that dizzies, eucharistic.

# Behind Closed Doors

With days like today
lashing the windows with rain
and flagellant winds that flay
the last yellow leaves from branches,
who needs discipline
from a slap, a spank, or a thong;
who needs bites and bruises,
the same old song and dance
of bandit mask and silver spur
to teach the pleasure
of total submission?
With days like today,
however others get their kicks,
now that November has come
who needs a dominatrix?

# Climacteric Collect

Late November, not a flower in sight,
Iceland poppy, Chinese delphinium,
Tuberous begonia, big-leaved hydrangea,
Lilac, lily, tulip, larkspur,
Zip, zilch, a big fat goose egg
On all those corollas, corollae,
Hibiscus, gloxinia, Cape jasmine gardenia,
And also its calyx, each and every
Pistil and stamen, long gone, amen,
Filament, anther, producer of pollen,
Usually unnoticed, and yet the very
Thread of the warp, thread of our life,
Sing it, amen, geranium, daisy, desert
Sand verbena, and in those distant places,
Tropics or tundra, where two or three
Stamens are gathered the plural is
Stamina, stamina, for which I'm crazy grateful,
Yellow star thistle, Purple owl's clover,
So ripped with thanksgiving for more than my share,
So ready to beg you for limitless more.

# December

Hangdog suns skulk in the south,
shirking the late afternoon.
It doesn't get darker than this.
Now what? What are we waiting for?
Doesn't get more naked either.
Not as in nude, posing on pillows
with just the right look
for cameras and easels,
but as in stripped of every stitch,
last oak leaves gone,
no hospital gown of snow.
What's next? Rasping impatience?
Or stiffening torpor, unstirred
by this face without makeup?
Or could it be catching the indigo eye
even the briefest sky bats,
reveler in expectation?

# The Shortest Day Has its Say

We need to talk,
said the solstice to the equinox.
You know I love how balanced you are,
how you tip toward neither night nor day;
you know I adore the way you rhyme
with fox, clocks, paradox,
while I can only fudge with pole-star,
gallstone, upholster. As for balance,
forget it; I'm the extreme standing of the sun,
north or south, in every year the flagrant zenith
or egregious nadir. But don't be afraid,
for if I'm nothing but blackest dark
at the cap of one hemisphere,
it's no sin or cause for medication,
since that very second at the other
I radiate completely. Undiluted. Sheer.
And in wavelengths available to the unaided eye.
Don't cry. I've also got two sides.
I just can't show you both.
Not in one place at one time.

# Night Sky over Norwalk, 1956

Think of it this way. If you like night sky,
you'll dig December in Connecticut,
and why not learn to love what's abundant?
A little simple math and we could discover
the phase of the moon, or better yet
let's just make it full. Does that help?
Well, yes, clouds could have covered it,
and we can check the records to learn
if altocumulus undulatus layered thick bands
between my mother and all lunar light.
But think of this. Even if the clouds
obscured the moon, even if the moon was new,
in either case, way above the flashing planes
still few in number, farther than the reach
of televised waves just beginning to lick
receptive antennae, out beyond the altitude
where the first satellite would orbit soon,
as the nearly longest night lay stretching out
its vast, black prairie, Virgo kept rising,
as did Pluto, rather rare, and no matter what
my mother hoped, the moon sat in Cancer,
and whatever my father planned while dozing off
over cooling coffee, Venus hung in Scorpio
and Venus must be honored.

# My Father's Study

Now that I'm six I stand before the floor-to-ceiling shelves and scan the top by bending back my neck, which never gets stiff, as though looking up a skyscraper's height, but none of the jackets and spines, purple with white words, black with red words, green with gold words, has much to say about how things will end.   The globe in the mahogany stand plugs in and lights up lots of countries with capitals to learn and names to sound out (*Eee-thee-o-pee-uh*), a glowing ball of mostly ocean-blue to spin whichever way one wants, not caring how the planet actually revolves or what conclusions it's turning toward much more quickly when spun too fast by someone disobedient, alone with its glow just before bedtime.  As for the ceiling where the rows of books all end, it's soundproof, so noise doesn't carry and words voiced aloud lose resonance, falling flat, as though deflated or drained of sap, even the mysterious beauties to come, the ones unlearned and still unsaid, like *dementia* and *dyskinesia*, each from a language no longer spoken around the shiny Mediterranean, which dizzies as it flashes past.

# After the Memorial Service

Light snow falls and doesn't think
how soon it will be gone;

branches whiten and never wonder
should it come to more than this;

and the junco, alighting, flicks
a few flakes from its feathers,

then hunts for seeds, not reasons
it isn't lessened by not lasting.

# Berries and Buds

Now without leaves,
what's our world

coming to but these
winter fruits,

so small and yet
the tiny lights

we hold up into
a vanishing sun:

red beads of the
Venus bush, rare,

yellow globes of
climbing willow vine,

very hard to find,
and the blue jewels

of sweet eye creeper,
each colorful cluster

with flesh enough
to see us through

this skinless season
of modest buds,

fuzzy to the touch,
which one warm day

will swell too much,
let loose, erupt.

Stephen Cushman is the author of two books of poems, both published by LSU, *Blue Pajamas* (1998) and *Cussing Lesson* (2002), as well as of two books of literary criticism and a book on the Civil War. He teaches at the University of Virginia.

Printed in the United States
56344LVS00004B/402

9 781933 456355